WHS

NATIONAL TESTS practice papers

FOR THE YEAR 2004

Maths, English and Science

Book 1 Levels 3–5

AGE 10–11
Key Stage 2

practice papers

Contents	Page
Introduction	
The National Tests: A Summary	iii
Maths Test	
Maths at Key Stage 2	1
Test A (without calculator)	2
Test B (with calculator)	11
Mental Maths Test	20
Answers	22
National Curriculum Levels	26
English Test	
Reading Test	27
Writing Test	43
Spelling Test	47
Answers	49
National Curriculum Levels	53
Science Test	
Science at Key Stage 2	54
Science Test	55
Answers	63
National Curriculum Levels	64

Acknowledgements
The authors and publisher would like to thank the following for permission to reproduce material in this book.

'Christmas Eve', from *Her Benny*, Silas Hocking, Memories Paperback, 1994
'They're Fetching in Ivy and Holly', from *Selected Poems for Children*, Charles Causley, John Laurence (illustrator), Macmillan Children's Books, 1997.

Every effort has been made to trace and acknowledge ownership of copyright material but if any have been inadvertently overlooked, the publisher will be pleased to make the necessary alterations at the first opportunity.

First published 2003
exclusively for WHSmith by
Hodder & Stoughton Educational,
a division of Hodder Headline Ltd
338 Euston Road
London NW1 3BH

Text © Hodder & Stoughton Educational 2003

All rights reserved. No part of this publication may be reproduced or transmitted in any form or by any means, electronic or mechanical, including photocopying, recording or any information storage and retrieval system, without permission in writing from the publisher.

A CIP record for this book is available from the British Library.

Authors: Steve Mills and Hilary Koll (Maths), Christine Moorcroft and Ray Barker (English), Graham Peacock (Science)

ISBN 0 340 81383 0

Impression   5 4 3 2 1
             2004 2003

Printed and bound by Hobbs The Printers, Totton, Hampshire

NOTE: The tests, questions and advice in this book are not reproductions of the official test materials sent to schools. The official testing process is supported by guidance and training for teachers in setting and marking tests and interpreting the results. The results achieved in the tests in this book may not be the same as those achieved in the official tests.

Introduction

The National Tests: A Summary

What are the National Tests?
Children who attend state schools in England and Wales sit National Tests (also known as SATs) at the ages of 7, 11 and 14, usually at the beginning of May. They may also sit optional tests in the intervening years – many schools have chosen to adopt these tests. The test results are accompanied by an assessment by the child's teacher.

The results are used by the school to assess each child's level of knowledge and progress in English and Maths at Key Stage 1 and English, Maths and Science at Key Stages 2 and 3. They also provide useful guidance for the child's next teacher.

The educational calendar for children aged 5–14 is structured as shown in the table alongside.

Key Stage	Year	Age by end of year	National Test
1 (KS1)	1	6	
	2	7	KEY STAGE 1
2 (KS2)	3	8	Optional Year 3
	4	9	Optional Year 4
	5	10	Optional Year 5
	6	11	KEY STAGE 2
3 (KS3)	7	12	
	8	13	
	9	14	KEY STAGE 3

Test Timetable
Key Stage 2 tests take place in one week in May. All children sit the same test at the same time. In 2004, the tests will take place in the week of **10–14 May**. Your child's school will be able to provide you with a detailed timetable.

Levels
National average levels have been set for children's results in the National Tests. The levels are as follows:

LEVEL	AGE 7 (Key Stage 1)	AGE 11 (Key Stage 2)	AGE 14 (Key Stage 3)
8			
7			
6			
5			
4			
3			
2			
2a			
2b			
2c			
1			

- BELOW EXPECTED LEVEL
- EXPECTED LEVEL
- ABOVE EXPECTED LEVEL
- EXCEPTIONAL

Results
Your child's school will send you a report indicating his or her levels in the tests and the teacher assessment.

The school's overall test results will be included in local and national league tables, which are published in most newspapers.

What can parents do to help?
While it is never a good idea to encourage cramming, you can help your child to succeed by:

- Making sure he or she has enough food, sleep and leisure time during the test period.
- Encouraging him or her to practise important skills such as writing and reading stories, spelling and mental arithmetic.
- Telling him or her what to expect in the test, such as important symbols and key words.
- Helping him or her to be comfortable in test conditions including working within a time limit, reading questions carefully and understanding different ways of answering.

Maths Test

Maths at Key Stage 2

The Key Stage 2 National Tests cover Number, Measures, Shape and Space, and Data Handling. Most children will take two one-hour written tests and a short, orally delivered mental test. Test A is a written non-calculator paper and Test B is a written paper where children can use a calculator, should they wish.

Levels

Children taking the Maths Tests A and B and the Mental Maths Test can achieve below level 3, level 3, level 4 or level 5, with a typical 11-year-old attaining level 4.

To gain an idea of the level at which your child is working, use the table on page 26, which shows you how to convert your child's marks into a National Curriculum level.

Setting the tests

Written tests

Allow one hour for each test. Do not expect your child to take them one after another. In the National Test week, children will take the mathematics tests over two or three days. Your child will need a ruler, pencil, rubber, protractor and, if possible, a small mirror or piece of tracing paper, together with a calculator (for Test B).

Encourage your child to work systematically through each test, returning later to questions which cause difficulty.

If your child has difficulty in reading the questions, you can read them aloud, provided the mathematical words are not altered or explained. Where necessary, your child can dictate answers and these can be written down for him or her. For large numbers, however, your child should be clear which digits are intended to be written, e.g. for a number such as three thousand and six your child should indicate that this is written as three, zero, zero, six.

Mental Maths Test

The mental test should take approximately 10–15 minutes to give, by reading aloud the questions on page 20, which you should copy for your own use while your child writes on page 21. Your child will only need a pencil and a rubber for the mental test.

Allow only the time suggested for each question. You may read each one twice within this time.

Marking the tests

Next to each question in the written tests is a number indicating how many marks the question or part of the question is worth. Enter your child's mark into the circle above this, using the answer pages to help you decide how many points to award.

Find your child's total score from the written tests and mental test, then refer to page 26 for information about the level your child might be working at.

Maths Test
Test A (without calculator)

1 Fill in the missing numbers.

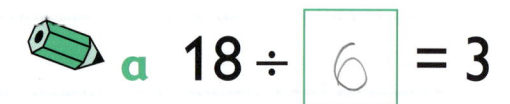

a 18 ÷ [6] = 3

b 12 + 15 = 38 − [11]

c (2 × 20) − [30] = 10 + [20]

2 Write two more numbers into this diagram so that the numbers in each row and column add up to 100.

(10) (60) (30)

(50) (20) (30)

(40) (20) (40)

3 a Continue this sequence.

3   4   6   9   [13]   [18]

b Explain how you worked out the missing numbers.

because it goes in the pattern of 1,2,3,4,5

TOTAL 6

Maths Test A

4 At a netball tournament there are 7 players in each team.

112 players take part in the tournament.

How many teams take part in the tournament?

16

5 Lucy is playing darts. She throws three darts and hits **three different** numbers. She notices that the **mean** of the numbers is **9**.

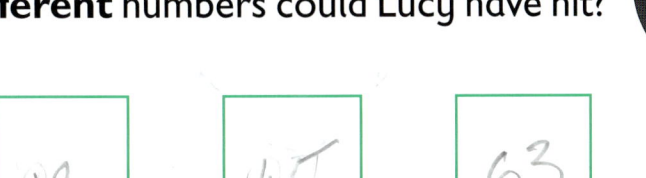

What **different** numbers could Lucy have hit?

| 18 | 45 | 63 |

Maths Test A

6 A shop sells ice cream.

This table shows the most popular types of ice cream sold in the shop during one day.

Flavour	Large cone	Small cone
Chocolate	15	14
Vanilla	19	12
Strawberry	11	8

29
31
19

a How many **large** cones were sold during the day?

45

1

b Which flavour was the most popular during the day?

Vanilla

1

7 One side of a shape has been drawn below. The shape has **three right angles** and **more than four sides**. Using a ruler, draw the other sides to complete the shape.

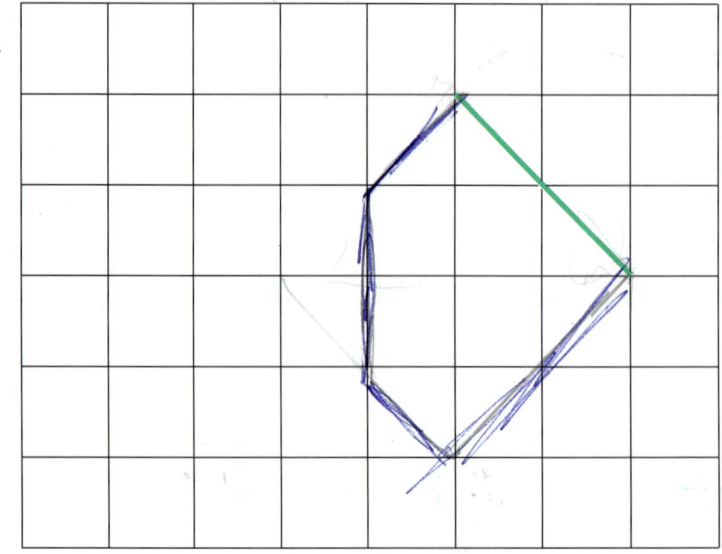

2

TOTAL

4

4

Maths Test A

8 Mr Thomas bought three shirts.

a One shirt cost £4.25. The second shirt cost twice as much.

How much did the second shirt cost?

£ 8.50

b Mr Thomas spent exactly £20 on all three shirts.

How much did the third shirt cost?

£ 7.25

9 Fill in the missing numbers so the numbers along all three sides have the same total.

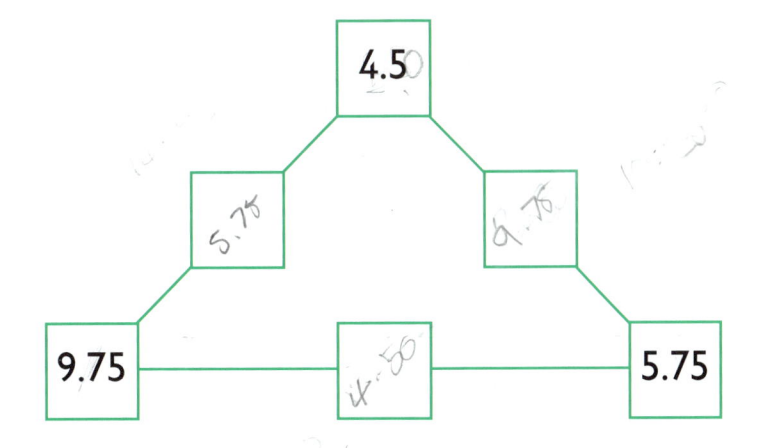

4.50

5.75

9.75   5.75

Maths Test A

10 Playing cards come in different suits.

diamonds   clubs   spades   hearts

Here are five playing cards.

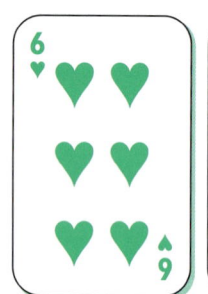

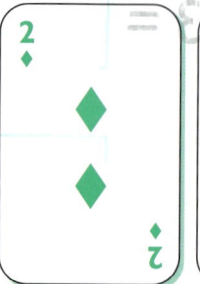

These five cards are shuffled and spread out face down on a table. **One card** is picked from them.

   a What is the probability that it is a **heart**? Give your answer as a fraction.

     1/4

   b What is the probability that it is a **diamond**? Show your answer by drawing a cross on this line.

     0 —————————— 1

11 The hundreds digits are missing from two numbers in this number sentence. Write what they could be.

     4 5 9 + 3 7 4 = 833

Maths Test A

12 Look at this multiplication fact.

$$26 \times 123 = 3198$$

Use this fact to find the answers to these questions:

a $25 \times 123 =$ 3197

b $26 \times 124 =$ 3208

c $260 \times 123 =$ 31980

d $2.6 \times 12.3 =$ 319.8

13 Circle **two** fractions below that are equivalent.

$\frac{2}{5}$ $\boxed{\frac{3}{8}}$ $\frac{6}{10}$ $\boxed{\frac{6}{16}}$

$\frac{6}{12}$ $\frac{1}{10}$ $\frac{6}{8}$

14 Calculate **952 − 436**   416

Maths Test A

15 a Using a ruler, and a mirror or tracing paper, **draw and shade** the reflection of the shape below in the mirror line.

1 cm

1 cm

a

mirror line

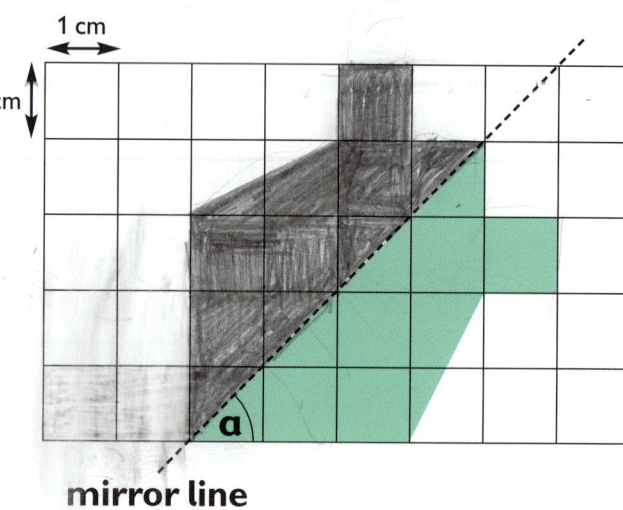

b What area of the grid is now shaded?   16 cm²

c What fraction of the grid is now shaded? $\frac{16}{40}$

d How many degrees is **angle a**? You may use an angle measurer (protractor).   45°

16 Here are two squares drawn on a graph.
Fill in the missing **co-ordinates** of **point C**.

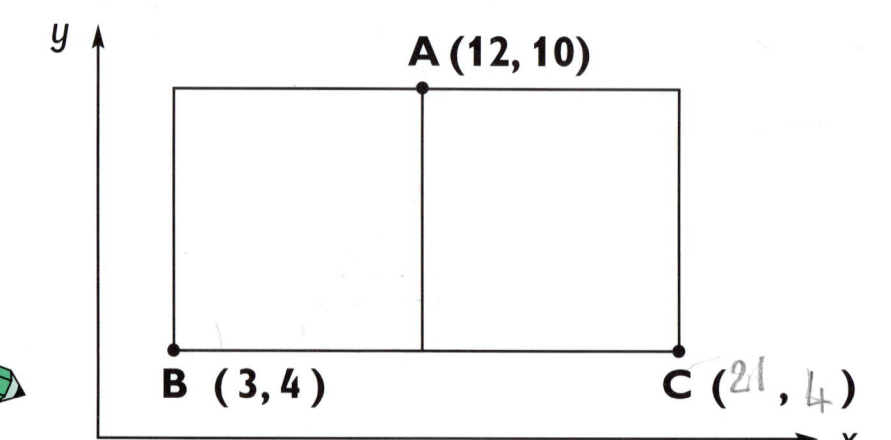

y

A (12, 10)

B (3, 4)   C (21, 4)

x

TOTAL 7

8

17 In a gymnastics competition, the gymnasts are awarded points for **difficulty**, **style** and **technical merit**. These points are added together to find a total score.

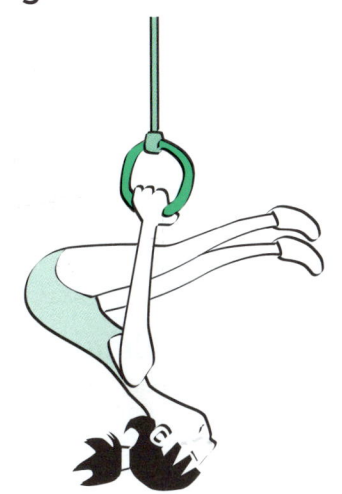

Here are the numbers of points awarded to three children.

Name	Difficulty	Style	Technical merit
Alice	3.8	5.1	4.7
Ajay	4.3	4.9	5.2
Emily	5.4	4.6	4.8

a What is the **total** number of points awarded to Emily?

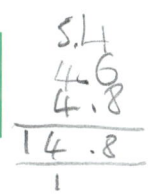

14.8

b For **difficulty**, who was awarded **closest** to 4 points?

Alice

c What was the difference between Emily's and Alice's **total** scores?

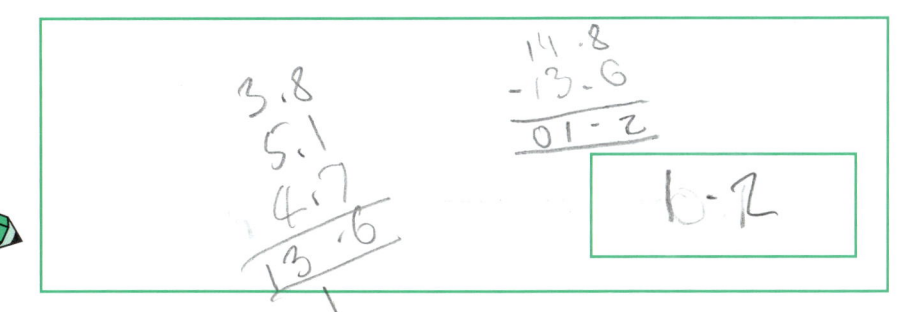

6.2

Maths Test A

18 Mrs Wood is buying some fruit.

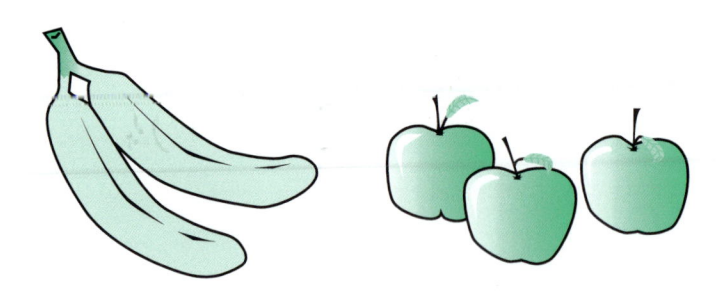

The fruit comes in bags of different sizes. This table shows the prices of the different bags.

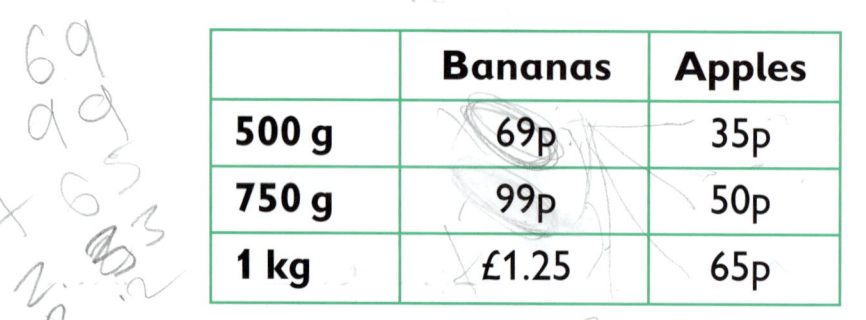

	Bananas	Apples
500 g	69p	35p
750 g	99p	50p
1 kg	£1.25	65p

Mrs Wood buys **three bags** of fruit. She buys **one** 500 g bag, **one** 750 g bag and **one** 1 kg bag.

a What is the total **mass** of fruit she buys?

£4.49

b She spends a total of **£2.33**.

Which **three** bags does she buy?

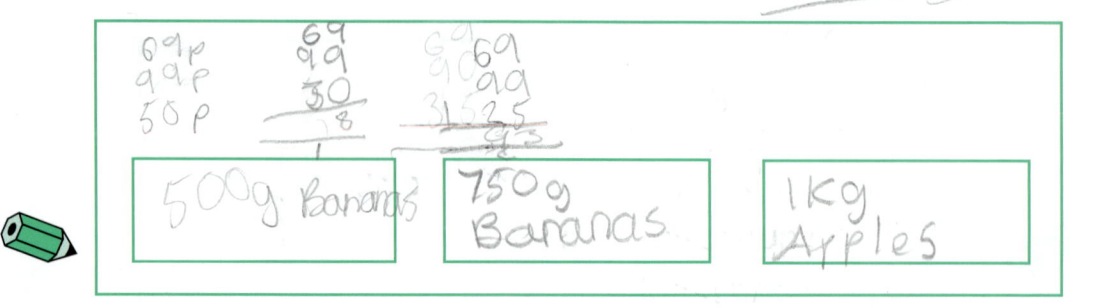

500g Bananas | 750g Bananas | 1kg Apples

Maths Test
Test B (with calculator)

1 Write three numbers to make the number sentence correct.

[52] + [50] + [2] = 104

2 An arrow is pointing to each of the number lines below.
Write the numbers indicated by the arrows into the boxes.

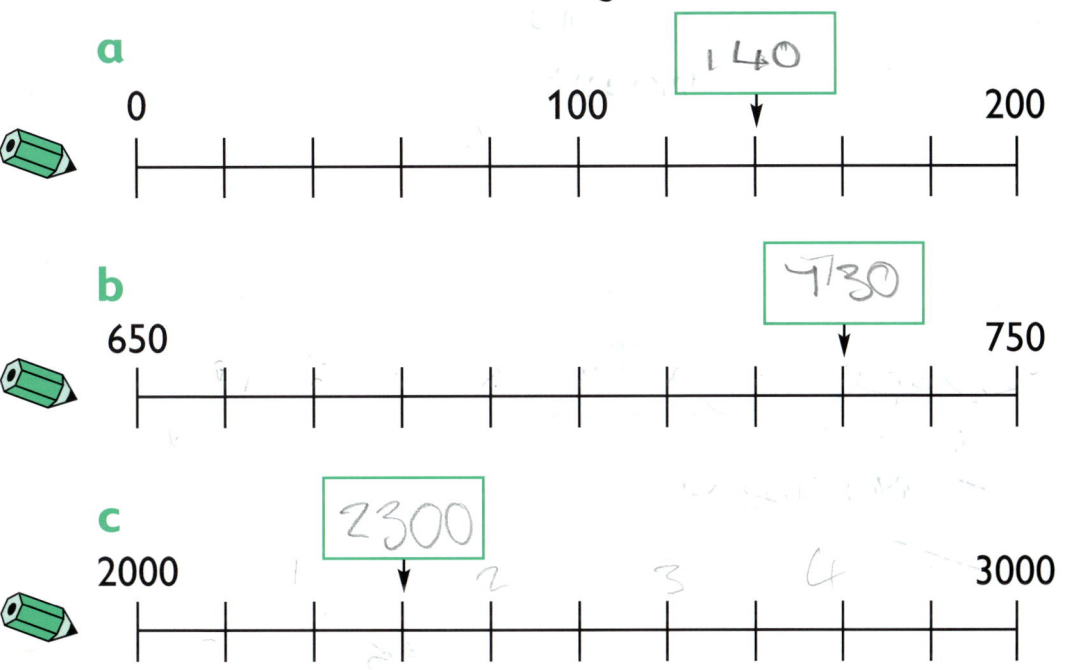

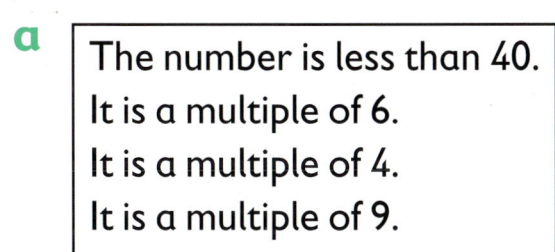

a [140]
0 — 100 — 200

b [730]
650 — 750

c [2300]
2000 — 3000

3 Here are some number riddles.
Write the number for each riddle in the box.

a The number is less than 40.
It is a multiple of 6.
It is a multiple of 4.
It is a multiple of 9.

[36]

b The number is between 30 and 50.
It is a square number.
It is an odd number.

[49]

Maths Test B

4 Write what the **missing numbers** could be to make the number sentences correct.

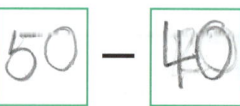

a [50] − [40] + [15] = 25

b [64] ÷ [8] = 8

c 5 × 3 + [15] = 6 × [ ]

5 **3781** people go to a football match.

They each pay **£3.50** to get in.

3781
£3.50
3781
3050

a What is the total amount of money paid?

£ [ ]

Programmes cost 75p each.

A **total** of **£604.50** is raised from selling programmes.

b How many programmes are sold?

12

Maths Test B

6 This diagram shows the **number of kilometres** between some cities in the United Kingdom.

	Aberdeen	Bristol	Glasgow	Manchester	Dover
Aberdeen	—	490	150	332	574
Bristol	490	—	366	167	195
Glasgow	150	366	—	210	467
Manchester	332	167	210	—	265
Dover	574	195	467	265	—

a Explain why each number appears twice in the table.

_____

_____

b A delivery driver visits three cities on the same journey. She starts at **Bristol**, drives to **Manchester** and then on to **Dover**. How far does she travel?

☐ km

7 Use all of these digits to make the four-digit number closest to 5000.

8 4 3 5

5348

Maths Test B

8 Here is an arrangement of dots. Join some of these dots with straight lines to draw a **regular hexagon**. Use a ruler.

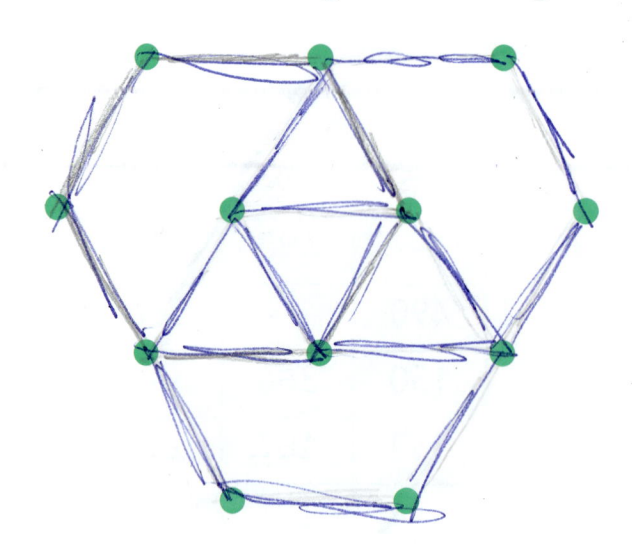

9 Hannah is colouring a flag.

The pattern she is colouring has **rotational symmetry**.

She still has **one square** to colour.

Shade **one** square so that the pattern will have **rotational symmetry**.

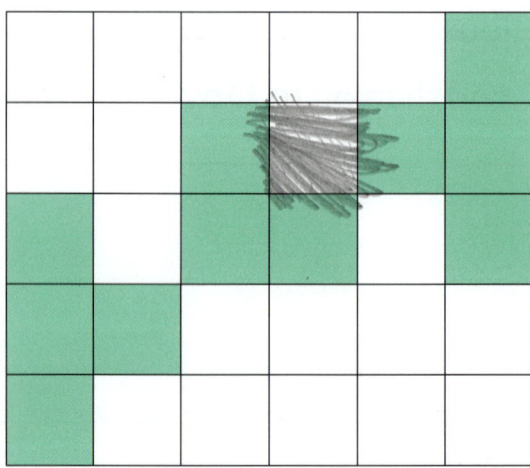

10 This number sequence is made by counting on in steps of **equal size**. Fill in the **missing numbers**.

4 ☐ ☐ 22 ☐

Maths Test B

11 David is playing a game using a set of ten **different** number cards showing **1 to 10**. He turns over two cards and adds the numbers to find the **total**.

These are his first four goes:

Card 1	Card 2	Total
6	7	13
3	5	8
4	9	13
7	2	9

a What is the **lowest total** David could possibly get?

b Jenny says,

"You are equally likely to get a total of 10 as a total of 3."

Is she correct?
Circle yes or no.

| yes | no |

Explain your answer.

_____

_____

_____

12 Fill in the missing numbers to make these statements correct.

a 53 912 ÷ ☐ = 586

b 5748 × ☐ = 120 708

Maths Test B

13 Look carefully at the shapes below.

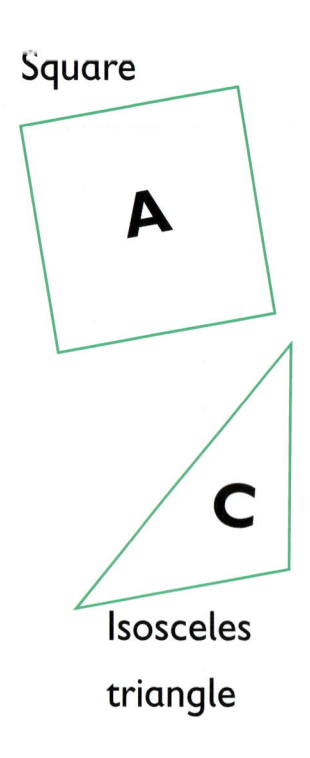

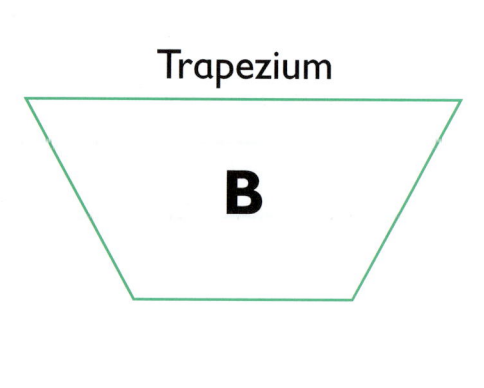

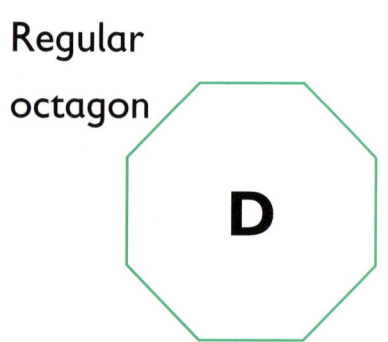

Square

Trapezium

A

B

Regular octagon

C

D

Isosceles triangle

Write the letter of shapes **B**, **C** and **D** into the correct section of the table below. **A** has been done for you.

	No pairs of parallel sides	One pair of parallel sides	More than one pair of parallel sides
3 sides			
4 sides			A
More than 4 sides			

14 Calculate 32% of 950.

Maths Test B

15 Mr Hall is making some blackcurrant drink.

He uses **125 ml** of blackcurrant squash and then fills the jug to the top with water.

a Use a ruler to draw a **line** to show where the **125 ml** of blackcurrant squash would come to on the **litre** container.

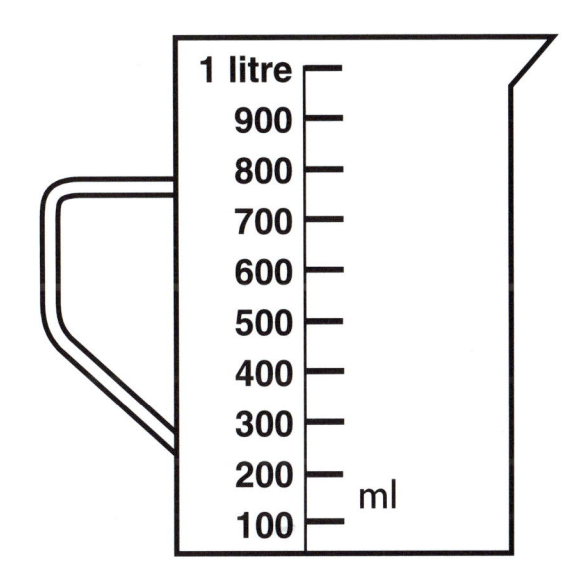

b How many times more water than blackcurrant squash does Mr Hall use?

c Mr Hall drinks **one-quarter** of the litre of blackcurrant drink. How much drink does he have now?

Give your answer in **litres**. ☐ l

17

Maths Test B

16 Carol is arranging exactly **four** number cards to make different fractions **less than one**. These are the numbers.

10 2 5 4

a Using **each** number card only **once**, show where each would go to make this statement correct.

☐/☐ is the same value as ☐/☐

b Find another way to place these cards to make **different** fractions that have the same value.

☐/☐ is the same value as ☐/☐

17 Here is part of a flower bed.

The flower bed has **16 rows** of daffodils. Each row has **17** daffodils in it. How many daffodils are there in **13** flower beds?

18 Jack and Chloe go to a car boot sale. They buy some books.

Entrance fee 75p and 20p for each book

a Jack pays the **entrance fee** and buys **twelve books**.

How much does he spend?

b Chloe pays the **entrance fee** and buys some books.

She spends exactly **£2.55**.

How many books does she buy?

Entrance fee 75p and 20p for each book

c Write a formula to show the total cost (**C**) in pence of visiting the car boot sale if you buy **n** books.

C =

Mental Maths Test
Questions

"For this first set of questions you have five seconds to work out each answer and write it down."

1. Write the number four thousand and nine in figures.
2. What is eighteen more than thirty?
3. What is twice one point seven?
4. Seven-tenths of the children in a class are boys. What percentage are boys?
5. How many sides do three octagons have in total?
6. What is half of seventy-two?

"For the next set of questions you have ten seconds to work out each answer and write it down."

7. What is double one hundred and eighty?
8. How many minutes are there in two and a half hours?
9. Add five and nineteen and then divide by three.
10. A snail crawls eighty-one centimetres. How much further does it have to crawl to reach one metre?
11. One-third of a number is seven. What is the number?
12. On the answer sheet is part of a scale. What number is the arrow pointing to?
13. A shop has a sale. All items are twenty-five per cent of their original price. A video costs four pounds in the sale. What was its original price?
14. Sam cycles six miles every day. How far does he cycle in a week?
15. Look at the answer sheet. Draw a ring around the approximate height of a door.

"For the next set of questions you have fifteen seconds to work out each answer and write it down."

16. Look at the answer sheet. Draw a ring around the number that is nearest to seven.
17. Thirty per cent of a number is fifteen. What is the number?
18. Which year is seventeen years before the year two thousand and two?
19. Look at the answer sheet. What is the size of angle A?
20. Look at the answer sheet. Draw a ring around three numbers that are multiples of twenty.

Mental Maths Test
Answer Sheet

5-second questions

1.
2.
3.
4.
5.
6.

10-second questions

7.
8. _____ minutes
9.
10. _____ centimetres
11.
12. [scale 4.6 to 4.7]
13. £
14. _____ miles
15. 2000 cm   20 m
    200 cm
    20 cm   2 cm

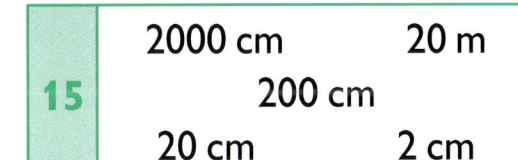

15-second questions

16. 0.7   7.9   6.6
    7.5   7.74
17.
18.
19. A= [triangle with 90°, 50°, A]
20. 240   130   290
    88   580   200

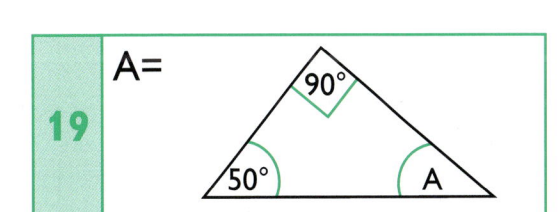

6

9

5

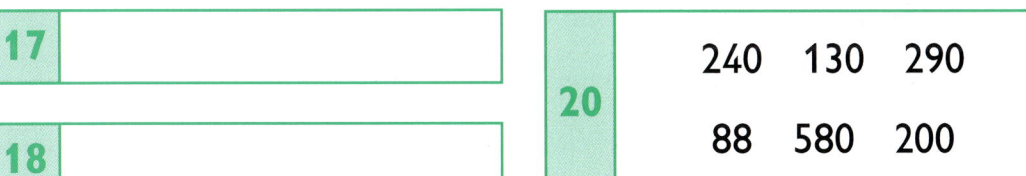

TOTAL
20

Answers
Maths Test

Question number	Answer	Mark	Parent's notes and additional information
TEST A			
1a	6	1	
1b	11	1	
1c	e.g. 10, 20	1	Two numbers to make the equation true.
2	20, 30	1	
3a	13, 18	1	
3b	A mark for either: an explanation that the differences between numbers in the sequence go up in ones or a reference to counting on, e.g. 'no numbers missed out, one number missed out, two numbers missed out, etc.'	1	Children's answers to questions like these should include <u>numbers</u> to support their explanations. Just writing 'I saw a pattern. The numbers go up' is generally not enough to score a mark.
4	112 ÷ 7 = 16	2	It does not matter whether this calculation is done mentally or using a written method. 1 mark for an attempt to divide 112 by 7.
5	Any three <u>different</u> numbers that have a total of 27, e.g. 8, 9, 10 or 20, 3, 4.	1	The mean (average) of a set of numbers is found by finding the total and dividing this by the number of numbers in the set. In this case there are 3 numbers so the mean is **27** ÷ 3 = **9**.
6a	45	1	Children are required to interpret the table and then find the total of 15, 19 and 11.
6b	vanilla	1	Children should check the total of each row to find the most popular flavour.
7	Any shape with more than 4 sides and with exactly 3 right angles. External right angles (those outside the shape) do not count.	2	Examples of shapes: 1 mark if the shape has more than 4 sides and some right angles.
8a	£8.50 Note that amounts of money should never be written with both the **£** sign and a **p** sign, e.g. £8.50p is incorrect and would not earn a mark.	1	Children must double £4.25. Children of this age should try to learn doubles of all numbers to 100 and their corresponding halves, e.g. double 25 = 50 and half of 50 = 25. They can then use this knowledge for questions of this kind.
8b	£7.25	1	
9	All three sides should have the same total.	2	
10a	$\frac{1}{5}$	1	There are 5 cards. The probability of picking the only heart is one out of five. Probabilities generally can be written in words or as fractions or decimals, e.g. **one out of five**, $\frac{1}{5}$ or **0.20**.
10b		1	There are 5 cards. The probability of picking one of the two diamonds is two out of five = 0.40.
11	Two digits that add to make 7, e.g. **1**59 + **6**74 **2**59 + **5**74 **3**59 + **4**74 **4**59 + **3**74 **5**59 + **2**74 or **6**59 + **1**74	1	If your child has written two digits that add to make 8, encourage him or her to add the two numbers together, e.g. 459 + 474 Point out that the answer comes to 933.
12a	3075	1	Your child should notice that 25 × 123 is 123 less than 26 × 123. Ideally he or she should subtract 123 from 3198 to get 3075. A mark can be awarded if the answer was found using a different method.
12b	3224	1	Again, your child should notice that 26 × 124 is 26 more than 26 × 123. If he or she finds this difficult, discuss it in a context, e.g. 124 things costing £26, cost £26 more than 123 things costing £26.

Maths Test Answers

Question number	Answer	Mark	Parent's notes and additional information
12c	31 980	1	This answer is ten times larger than the given multiplication fact.
12d	31.98	1	Encourage your child to work out an approximate answer to decide where the decimal point should go, e.g. **2.6** × **12.3** is approximately **3** × **12** = 36, so the answer is not 319.8 or 3.198, but 31.98.
13	$\frac{3}{8}$ and $\frac{6}{16}$ are equivalent.	1	Equivalent means that the fractions have the same value, e.g. if you have $\frac{3}{8}$ of a pizza it is the same value as $\frac{6}{16}$ of a pizza.
14	516	1	
15a		2	1 mark should be awarded if 5 or 6 out of the 7 corners of the shape are reflected correctly.
15b	16 cm²	1	The area of a shape is the number of whole squares inside the shape. In this case it is centimetre squares or cm² that are counted. If your child gave the answer 22, he or she counted half squares as whole squares.
15c	$\frac{16}{40}$ or $\frac{8}{20}$ or $\frac{4}{10}$ or $\frac{2}{5}$	1	There should be 16 out of 40 squares shaded.
15d	45° Accept answers that are 1 degree either side of 45°, i.e. 44° or 46°.	1	A protractor is not essential for this question. Show your child that the angle is half a right angle and that the exact answer is 90 ÷ 2 = 45°.
16	(21, 4)	2	Award 1 mark for each co-ordinate. The second co-ordinate (how many up) is the same as B, i.e. 4. To work out the first co-ordinate (how far across) find the difference between 3 and 12 = 9 and then add this to 12 to get 21.
17a	14.8	1	5.4 + 4.6 + 4.8
17b	Alice Accept the answer 3.8.	1	Children may incorrectly answer 4.3. Show that 3.8 is two-tenths away from 4 whereas 4.3 is three-tenths away from 4.
17c	1.2	2	5.4 + 4.6 + 4.8 = 14.8 3.8 + 5.1 + 4.7 = <u>13.6</u> 1.2 Award 1 mark for workings that include an attempt to add Alice's scores and Emily's scores and to subtract one from the other.
18a	2250 g or 2.25 kg	1	500 g + 750 g + 1 kg (1000 g)
18b	500 g bananas (69p), 750 g bananas (99p), 1 kg apples (65p).	2	This question involves interpreting information and dealing with two criteria: the price (£2.33) and the different masses of the bags. Award 1 mark for attempts to add sets of three numbers, including prices and masses.
TEST B			
1	Any three numbers that add to make 104.	1	
2a	140	1	Show your child that each 100 is split into 5 sections, so each must be worth 20.
2b	730	1	Show your child that each 100 is split into 10 sections, so each must be worth 10.
2c	2300	1	Show your child that each 1000 is split into 10 sections, so each must be worth 100.
3a	36	1	A multiple is a number that can be divided exactly into without a remainder, e.g. multiples of 6 include 6, 12, 18, 180, 486, etc.
3b	49	1	A square number is a number that is made from multiplying another number by itself, e.g. 4 = 2 × 2, 9 = 3 × 3, 25 = 5 × 5. Children should learn the square numbers to 100, i.e. 1, 4, 9, 16, 25, 36, 49, 64, 81, 100.

23

Maths Test Answers

Question number	Answer	Mark	Parent's notes and additional information
4a	Any three numbers that make 25, e.g. 50 − 30 + 5, 100 − 80 + 5.	1	
4b	Any numbers that divide to make 8, e.g. 8 ÷ 1, 16 ÷ 2, 24 ÷ 3, 80 ÷ 10.	1	
4c	Any numbers that make the statement correct, e.g. 5 × 3 + **3** = 6 × **3** 5 × 3 + **9** = 6 × **4** 5 × 3 + **15** = 6 × **5**.	1	Children often find this type of question difficult as they see the equals sign as an 'answer giver' rather than meaning 'is/has the same answer as'. Here 5 × 3 + ☐ 'has the same answer as' 6 × ☐. Also, 5 × 3 must be multiplied before adding the missing number.
5a	£13 233.50 Do <u>not</u> award a mark for the answer <u>£13 233.5</u> or <u>£13 233.50**p**</u>	1	Money answers must be written correctly for questions of this type. Calculator questions like these are often selected to see whether children can interpret the display in the context of money. Amounts of money should never be written with both the **£** sign and a **p** sign.
5b	806	2	Here children must change the amounts of money to be either in pounds or in pence. If your child has given the answer 8.06 by dividing £604.50 by 75 <u>pounds</u>, point out that the ticket price is given in pence and needs to be altered to £0.75. Award 1 mark if your child has shown that he or she is trying to divide in pounds or in pence, e.g. £604.50 ÷ £0.75 or 60 450p ÷ 75p.
6a	Any explanation showing that your child appreciates that the distance between two towns, e.g. Bristol to Dover, will be the same distance in reverse, e.g. Dover to Bristol.	1	
6b	432 km	2	A common mistake is to select the incorrect second distance. If your child answered 362 km, it is because he or she used the distances between Bristol and Manchester (167) and then between <u>Bristol</u> and Dover (195), rather than Bristol and Manchester (167) and on from <u>Manchester</u> to Dover (265). Award 1 mark if the working shows 167 + 265 with an incorrect answer.
7	4853	1	
8	A regular hexagon has 6 equal sides and 6 equal angles.	1	
9		1	Shapes or patterns that have rotational symmetry can look the same in more than one orientation when turned. Letters like S, H, X, O have rotational symmetry, but A, E, T, W do not. They cannot be turned to look the same in any other orientation.
10	10, 16, 28	1	To answer this question, your child should find the difference between 22 and 4 = 18. If the difference between boxes that are three apart is 18 then the difference between each box is 18 ÷ 3 = 6.
11a	3	1	David can pick a 1 and a 2 card, with a total of 3.
11b	no There must be an explanation with reference to the fact that there are more ways to make 10 than there are to make 3, e.g. 3 can only be scored with a 1 and a 2 card, whereas 10 can be scored with a 1 and 9, 2 and 8, 3 and 7, 6 and 4, etc.	1	Children's answers to questions like these should include <u>numbers</u>, where possible. It is not enough to say that 'it is more likely to score 10 than 3'.
12a	92	1	Children often attempt questions of this type using trial and error, e.g. trying to divide 53 912 by different numbers to get 586. This involves a great deal of time. Instead, encourage your child to see that division questions can be rearranged, e.g. 10 ÷ 5 = 2 and 10 ÷ 2 = 5. Here children should divide 53 912 by 586 to get 92.
12b	21	1	Again, children attempt questions of this type using trial and error, e.g. trying to multiply 5748 by different numbers to get 12 0708. Instead, encourage your child to see that multiplication questions can be rearranged, e.g. 2 × 5 = 10 can be rearranged to make 10 ÷ 2 = 5. Here children should divide 12 0708 by 5748 to get 21.

Maths Test Answers

Question number	Answer	Mark	Parent's notes and additional information
13	C in top-left area; B and A in middle row (B left of A); D in bottom-right area	3	Parallel lines are lines that if extended in either direction would never meet. Parallel lines are the same distance apart. A regular shape has equal sides and equal angles. Award 1 mark for each of the letters B, C and D correctly positioned.
14	304	1	32% of 950 can be worked out in the following ways: $32 \div 100 \times 950$ or $32 \times 950 \div 100$ or 0.32×950
15a	Jug showing level at 125 ml (quarter between 100 and 200)	1	Show children that the litre jug (1000 ml) is split into 10 sections, so each must be worth 100, so 125 will come a quarter of the way between 100 and 200.
15b	7	2	Marks are awarded for the correct answer, whatever the method. Award 1 mark if the working shows an attempt to subtract 125 ml from 1 litre and divide by 125 with an incorrect answer.
15c	0.75 l	1	
16a	$\frac{4}{10}$ and $\frac{2}{5}$ or $\frac{2}{4}$ and $\frac{5}{10}$	1	The fractions can be in any order, e.g. $\frac{2}{5}$ and $\frac{4}{10}$ or $\frac{4}{10}$ and $\frac{2}{5}$
16b	$\frac{4}{10}$ and $\frac{2}{5}$ or $\frac{2}{4}$ and $\frac{5}{10}$	1	Do **not** award a mark if the answer has the same fractions as question 16a, even if given in a different order.
17	3536	2	Award 1 mark for a method that shows $16 \times 17 \times 13$ with an incorrect answer.
18a	£3.15 Do **not** award a mark for the answer £3.15**p** or **£315**.	1	Money answers must be written correctly for questions of this type. Calculator questions like these are often selected to see whether children can interpret the display in the context of money. Amounts of money should never be written with both the £ sign and a p sign.
18b	9	2	Children may incorrectly answer 12.75 or 13. Remind them that the entrance fee (75p) should be subtracted first. Award 1 mark for attempts to subtract 75 from 255 and divide this by 20.
18c	Any of the following answers: $C = 75 + (20 \times n)$ $C = 75 + (n \times 20)$ $C = 75 + 20n$ $C = 20n + 75$ $C = 20 \times n + 75$ etc. Award 1 mark for $C = 20n$ or $C = 20 \times n$	2	Children find using letters in place of numbers quite difficult. Show them the following: For 1 book C (cost) $= 75 + (1 \times 20)$ For 2 books C (cost) $= 75 + (2 \times 20)$ For 3 books C (cost) $= 75 + (3 \times 20)$, etc. So for n books C (cost) $= 75 + (n \times 20)$.

Mental Maths Test Answers

1. 4009
2. 48
3. 3.4
4. 70%
5. 24
6. 36
7. 360
8. 150
9. 8
10. 19 cm
11. 21
12. 4.67
13. £16
14. 42 miles
15. 200 cm
16. 6.6
17. 50
18. 1985
19. 40°
20. 240, 580, 200

One mark per correct answer.

25

National Curriculum Levels
Maths

Write your child's scores below.

Mark scored in Test A [ ] Maximum marks 40

Mark scored in Test B [ ] Maximum marks 40

Mark scored in Mental Test [ ] Maximum marks 20

Total score [ ] Maximum marks 100

The National Tests are levelled according to the child's total score.

Mark	24 or below	25–51	52–79	80–100
Level	Level 1/2	Level 3	Level 4	Level 5

For each test this can be broadly broken down as follows:

TEST A	Mark	0–10	11–20	21–31	32–40
	Level	Level 1/2	Level 3	Level 4	Level 5

TEST B	Mark	0–10	11–20	21–31	32–40
	Level	Level 1/2	Level 3	Level 4	Level 5

MENTAL TEST	Mark	0–4	5–10	11–15	16–20
	Level	Level 1/2	Level 3	Level 4	Level 5

If your child needs more practice in any Maths topics, use the WHSmith Key Stage 2 Maths Revision Guide.

English Test
Reading Test

The Reading Test at Key Stage 2 comprises a variety of texts – non-fiction, fiction and poetry – to test reading strategies across a range of genres. There will normally be a common theme.

The questions require four different kinds of answer:
- Short words or phrases (one mark for each correct response).
- Longer answers (one or two sentences) which require more understanding of the text (two marks).
- Detailed explanations of opinion (up to three marks).
- Multiple choice (one mark).

Although some questions will have a 'right answer', all children will express their responses in a different way.

Setting the test

> Allow 15 minutes for reading the passages and 45 minutes for answering the questions.

1. Encourage your child to read each passage carefully.
2. Point out the different types of question: those which give a choice of answers to tick and those which need a written answer. Written answers need not be complete sentences. Some written answers are worth three or more marks if detail or examples are required.
3. Do not help your child to read the text, although you may help with the spelling of the answers.
4. Point out that your child may rub out or alter any mistakes.
5. Tell your child:
   - to find the answers in the text, rather than guessing;
   - to tick only one box in multiple choice questions;
   - to try to answer every question;
   - to leave any questions he or she cannot answer and go back to them at the end;
   - to re-read the text to find the answers.

Reading Test

Different views of Christmas

Contents

Information: **Christmas Celebrations**

From a novel: **'Christmas Eve', from *Her Benny***

Poem: **'They're Fetching in Ivy and Holly'**

Christmas means different things to different people.

In these extracts, we look at different people's experiences and views of Christmas:

- from an information text about what Christmas means to Christians (a website to which people from different countries sent information);

- from a novel set about 130 years ago;

- from a twentieth-century poem.

You have **15 minutes** to read through these three passages, and **45 minutes** to answer the questions.

Christmas Celebrations

People around the world celebrate Christmas in different ways, both religious and non-religious. Many celebrations are based on legends and traditions which pre-date Christianity, and important dates in the Christian calendar (such as Epiphany, on 6 January) are sometimes linked with the dates of pagan festivals. Many celebrations include the traditional foods of a country and many are influenced by the climate of the country.

Mexico

As Christmas approaches, elaborately decorated market stalls are set up in town centres to sell crafts, foods such as cheese, bananas, nuts and cookies, and flowers such as orchids and poinsettias.

There is a legend about the poinsettia. A little boy gathered some green branches from along the roadside while he was walking to church to look at the Nativity scene (the birth of Jesus). Other children laughed when he laid them by the manger as an offering, but they fell silent when a brilliant red, star-shaped flower appeared on each branch.

Processions which enact Joseph and Mary's search for somewhere to stay in Bethlehem on the night Jesus was born begin nine days before Christmas, because Mary and Joseph's journey from Nazareth to Bethlehem took nine days. People form two groups: pilgrims and innkeepers. The pilgrims trudge from house to house asking for shelter. The innkeepers turn them away until they reach the house in which an altar and Nativity scene have been set up. They go in with great rejoicing, a traditional prayer is spoken, and the party begins.

Sweden

The 'Yule log' comes from Scandinavia. Traditions concerned with warmth and light arose because of the long, dark, cold winters. Yuletide means 'the turning of the sun' (the winter solstice). It was traditionally a time when fortunes for the coming year were determined and when the dead were thought to walk the earth.

Originally an entire tree was brought into the house with great ceremony. The bottom of the trunk was set into the hearth so that the rest of the tree stuck out into the room. It was burned until 6 January (the end of Yule).

A thousand years ago in Sweden, the King declared that Christmas would last a month, from the Feast of Saint Lucia (13 December) until Saint Knut's Day (13 January). Lucia was a 4th-century Sicilian saint and martyr who took food to Christians hiding from persecution in dark underground tunnels. To light the way she wore a wreath of candles on her head. She was discovered and killed. It is not known why she came to be revered in Sweden. Schools, businesses and communities sponsor processions of girls wearing white dresses and wreaths of candles; carols are sung and the Queen of Light is thanked for bringing hope at the darkest time of the year.

On Christmas Eve a Christmas gnome emerges from his home under the floor of the house or the barn. He brings a sack of gifts.

Reading Test

Nicaragua

In Nicaragua, Christmas begins on 7 December with *La Griteria* (The Calling), when groups of people call at each house in the neighbourhood singing joyful hymns to the Virgin Mary. The singers are given sweets and other small gifts. A giant doll, *La Gigantona* (The Female Giant), a symbol of Mary, is paraded dancing through the streets to the accompaniment of drums.

Japan

Christmas became popular in Japan at the beginning of the 20th century because of the Christmas products made there for other countries. It is a non-religious holiday devoted to children, and is celebrated mainly in cities.

Tinsel and lights are hung in dance halls, cafés and pinball parlours. Trees are decorated with small toys, dolls, gold paper fans and lanterns, wind chimes, candles and paper ornaments including origami swans.

Japanese children call Santa 'Santa Kuroshu'. He is believed to have eyes in the back of his head – to watch the children all year long!

Jamaica

On Christmas morning, processions of *jonkonoo* (masked dancing men) parade down the streets, beating drums to herald Christmas Day.

Ghana

In Ghana, Christmas celebrations go on for eight days. Children are given new clothes and other gifts. Bells ring all morning to call people to church.

The main dish for Christmas Day dinner is usually made from a fowl, goat or sheep. Yams and a soup made of meat and eggs are served.

In most towns, groups of children go from house to house, singing or chanting and blowing home-made trumpets throughout the eight days.

Iceland

Icelandic tradition has thirteen *Jolasveinar* (Christmas elves). Jolasveinar first appeared in the 17th century – the sons of the ogres Gryla and Leppaludi, who themselves had appeared in the 13th century and were said to have stolen and eaten naughty children.

The Jolasveinar live in mountains and start to arrive in towns, one a day, thirteen days before Christmas Eve, with the last one arriving that morning. As their names suggest, the Jolasveinar are playful imps who steal the seasonal food and play tricks: Door Slammer awakens sleepers by slamming doors; Candle Beggar snatches candles; and Meat Hooker tries to run off with the roast.

They also leave presents for children (in shoes the children have left on the windowsill the night before). If any children have been naughty, they leave a potato or some other reminder to be good. They start departing for home on Christmas Day, with the last one departing on Twelfth Night (6 January).

Reading Test

1 In which four countries are there special Christmas processions?

_____

_____

2 Which of the processions are linked with the Nativity?

_____

_____

What tells you this?

_____

_____

_____

_____

3 Which country's Christmas celebrations have arisen because of the weather or climate there?

_____

4 Give three examples of Christmas celebrations which are based on legends not connected with the Nativity.

_____

_____

_____

TOTAL 10

Reading Test

5 What is the main similarity between Christmas celebrations in Sweden and Iceland?

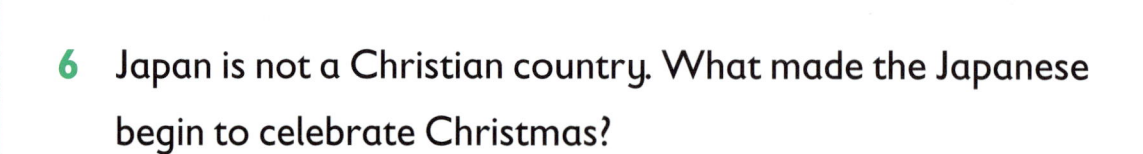

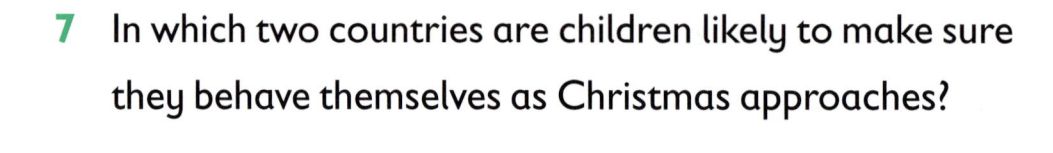

_____

_____

_____

6 Japan is not a Christian country. What made the Japanese begin to celebrate Christmas?

_____

_____

_____

7 In which two countries are children likely to make sure they behave themselves as Christmas approaches?

_____

_____

Explain your answer.

_____

_____

_____

_____

8 In which country does the Christmas season begin the earliest?

_____

9 In Sweden, what is the link between Saint Lucia and yuletide festivals?

_____
_____
_____
_____

10 Which traditional festivals, in which countries, are linked with the date of the Christian festival of Epiphany?

_____
_____
_____

Reading Test
Fiction

'Christmas Eve' from *Her Benny* by Silas Hocking

This book is set in Liverpool in the 1870s. Benny is ten and Nelly is nine years old. They make a living by selling matches. Benny also carries people's bags to and from the ferry-boats.

On Christmas Eve Benny took his sister through St John's Market, and highly delighted they were with what they saw. The thousands of geese, turkeys and pheasants, the loads of vegetables, the heaps of oranges and apples, the pyramids of every other conceivable kind of fruit, the stalls of sweetmeats, the tons of toffee, and the crowds of well-dressed people all bent upon buying something, were sources of infinite pleasure to the children. There was only one drawback to their happiness – they did not know how to lay out the sixpence they had brought with them to spend. If there had been less variety there would have been less difficulty; but, as it was, Benny felt as if he would never be able to decide what to buy. However, they agreed at last to lay out twopence for two slices of bread and ham, for they were both rather hungry; and then they spent the other fourpence on apples, oranges and toffee and, on the whole, felt very well satisfied with the result of their outlay.

It was rather later than usual when they got home, but old Betty knew where they had gone and, as it was Christmas Eve, she had got a bigger fire in than usual and had also got them a cup of hot cocoa each and some bunloaf to eat with it.

"By golly!" said Benny, as he munched the cake, "I do wish folks 'ud 'ave Christmas ev'ry week."

"You are a curious boy," said the old woman, looking up with a smile on her wrinkled face.

"Is I, Granny? I specks it's in my blood, as the chap said o' his timber leg."

The old woman had told them on the first evening of their arrival, when they had seemed at a loss what name to give her, to call her 'Granny'; and no name could have been more appropriate, or have come more readily to the children's lips.

"But could folks 'ave Christmas any oftener if they wished to?" asked little Nell.

"Of course they could, Nell," burst out Benny. "You dunna seem to know what folks make Christmas for."

"An' I thinks you dunno either, Benny."

"Don't I, though?" he said, putting on an air of importance. "It's made to give folks the chance of doing a lot o' feeding; didn't yer see all the gooses an' other nice things in the market that folks is going to polish off tomorrow?"

"I dunna think it was made purpose for that. Wur it now, Granny?"

Thus appealed to, the old woman, who had listened with an amused smile on her face, answered, "No, my child. It's called Christmas because it is the birthday of Christ."

"Who's he?" said Benny, looking up, while Nelly's eyes echoed the enquiry.

"Don't you know – ain't you never heerd?" said the old woman in a tone of surprise.

"Nay," said Benny, "nuthin' sense."

"Poor little dears! I didn't know as how you was so ignorant, or I should have told you before." And the old woman looked as if she did not know where or how to begin to tell the children the wonderful story, and for a considerable time remained silent. At length she said, "I'll read it to 'ee out o' the Book; mebbe you'll understand it better that way nor any way else."

And, taking down from a shelf her big and much-worn Bible, she opened it and began to read:

"Now when Jesus was born in Bethlehem of Judea …" And slowly the old woman read on until she reached the end of the chapter, while the children listened with wide and wondering eyes. To Nelly the words seemed like a revelation, responding to the deepest feeling in her nature, and awakening thoughts within her that were too big for utterance. Benny, however, could see nothing particularly interesting in the narrative itself. But the art of reading was to him a mystery past all comprehension. How Granny could see that story upon the pages of her Bible was altogether beyond his grasp. At length, after scratching his head vigorously for some time, he burst out:

"By jabbers! I's got it at last! Jimmy Jones squeeze me if I ain't! It's the specks that does it!"

"Does what?" said Nelly.

"Why, the story bizness, to be sure. Let me look at the book through your specks, shall I, Granny?"

"Ay, if you like, Benny." And the next minute he was looking at the Bible with Granny's spectacles astride his nose and an expression of disappointment upon his face.

"Golly! I's sold!" was his exclamation. "But this are a poser, and no mistake."

"What's such a poser?" said Granny.

"Why, how yer find the story in the book; for I can see nowt."

Reading Test

1 What made it difficult for the children to spend their sixpence?

| everything cost more than sixpence | they had to hurry because it was late | there was too much choice | they didn't see anything they wanted |

2 Who was old Betty?

| the children's grandmother | the person they lived with | their mother | their neighbour |

3 What impressed Benny most about Christmas?

| the food | it was Christ's birthday | the snow | the money people spent |

4 What surprised old Betty?

| the amount of food the children ate | they had money to spend | they were late coming home | they didn't know who Christ was |

5 Why was Betty silent for quite a long time?

| she didn't know how or where to begin telling them the story of Christ | she was speechless at their ignorance | the children were arguing about what Christmas was for | she was day-dreaming |

6 What does Benny mean by 'I specks'?

| a pair of glasses | the text on a page | I expect | my place |

TOTAL 6

36

Reading Test

7 Do you think the children go to school?

_____

How can you tell?

_____

_____

[2]

8 List three different exclamations of surprise used by Benny.

_____

_____

_____

[3]

9 What does Benny mean by 'Jimmy Jones squeeze me if I ain't'?

_____

_____

_____

_____

[1]

10 From the dialogue, give:

four examples in which verbs and pronouns do not agree

_____   _____

_____   _____

a non-standard plural _____

a non-standard past tense _____

a double negative _____

[5]

TOTAL

11

37

Reading Test

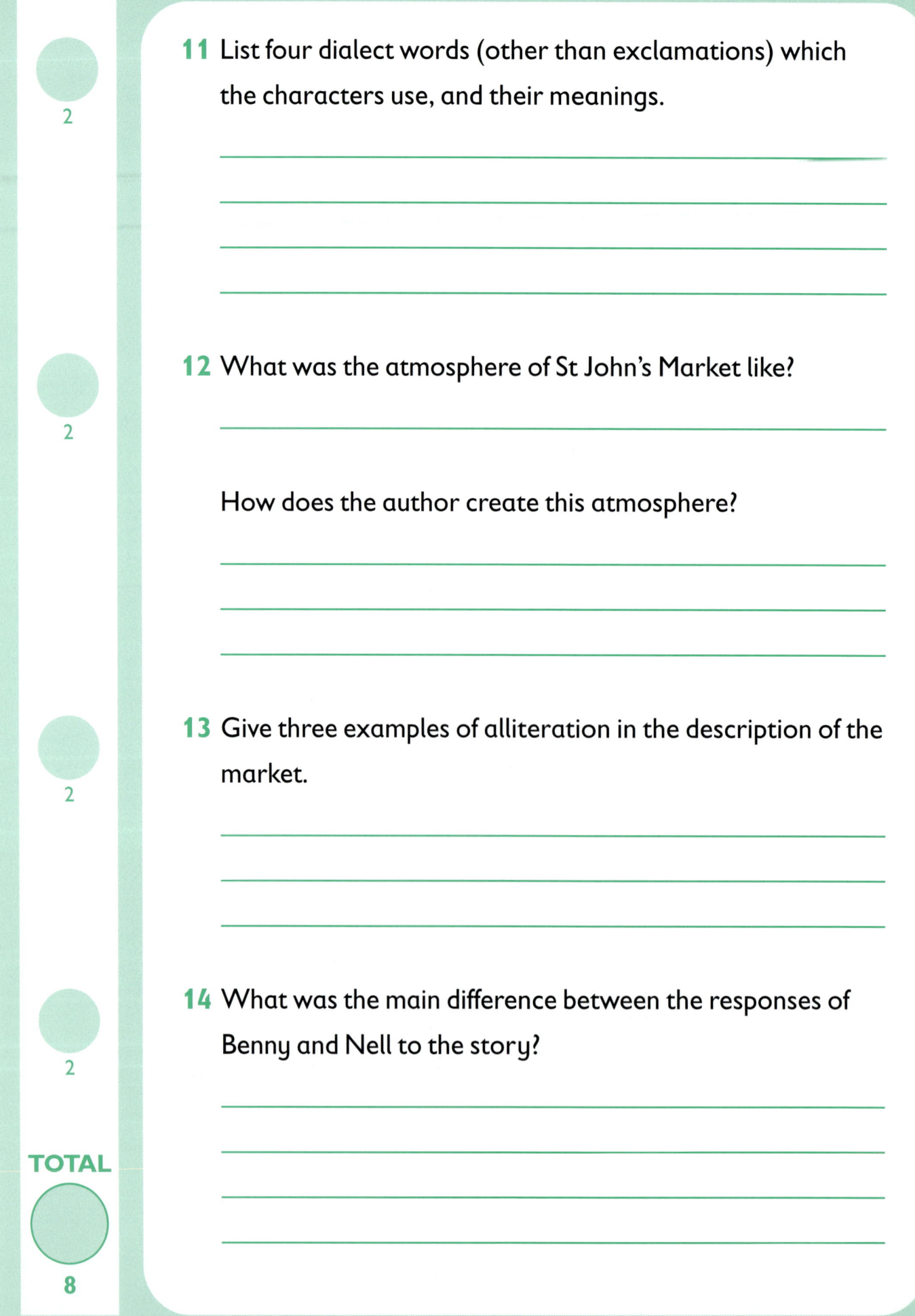

11 List four dialect words (other than exclamations) which the characters use, and their meanings.

_____

_____

_____

_____

12 What was the atmosphere of St John's Market like?

_____

How does the author create this atmosphere?

_____

_____

_____

13 Give three examples of alliteration in the description of the market.

_____

_____

_____

14 What was the main difference between the responses of Benny and Nell to the story?

_____

_____

_____

_____

TOTAL 8

38

Reading Test

15 How does the author help the reader to imagine the characters' accents?

_____

_____

Give four examples.

_____   _____

_____   _____

16 What can you tell about the narrator's religious beliefs?

_____

How can you tell?

_____

_____

_____

_____

_____

_____

Reading Test
Poetry

They're Fetching in Ivy and Holly

"They're fetching in ivy and holly
And putting it this way and that.
I simply can't think of the reason,"
Said Si-Si the Siamese cat.

"They're pinning up lanterns and streamers.
There's mistletoe over the door.
They've brought in a tree from the garden.
I do wish I knew what it's for.

"It's covered with little glass candles
That go on and off without stop.
They've put it to stand in a corner
And tied up a fairy on top.

"They're stringing bright cards by the dozen
And letting them hang in a row.
Some people outside in the roadway
Are singing a song in the snow.

"I saw all the children write letters
And – I'm not sure this was wise –
They posted each one *up the chimney*.
I couldn't believe my own eyes.

"What on earth, in the middle of winter,
Does the family think it is at?
Won't somebody come and tell me?"
Said Si-Si the Siamese cat.

Charles Causley

Reading Test

1 How can you tell that this poem is about Christmas? Give three examples which tell you this.

_____
_____
_____

3

2 Does Si-Si the cat think there must be a reason for the unusual goings-on?

_____

How can you tell?

_____
_____
_____

3

3 What amazes the cat most of all?

_____
_____
_____

1

4 Give three examples of lines which express the cat's puzzlement.

_____
_____
_____

3

TOTAL

10

41

Reading Test

5 What does this poem have to do with the Christian view of Christmas? Explain your answer.

_____
_____
_____

6 What do you think the poet is saying about the way in which people celebrate Christmas?

_____
_____
_____
_____

English Test
Writing Test

This test helps you to gain an insight into your child's ability to write independently and to communicate meaning to the reader using the conventions of punctuation, spelling and handwriting.

At Key Stage 2 children's writing is assessed through two Writing Tasks:

- a Longer Writing Task (45 minutes)
- a Shorter Writing Task (20 minutes).

Schools will be told what type of writing tasks to set but the topic is up to the teacher, who will take into account the interest and experience of the class. One Writing Task will be based on **fiction** and the other on **non-fiction**.

Children should be allowed time to plan their writing for both tasks, which they should not do one after the other.

The **Longer Task** is assessed for: **Sentence structure and punctuation** (up to 8 marks), **Text structure and organisation** (up to 8 marks) and **Composition and effect** (up to 12 marks). (Total 28 marks.)

Sentence structure and punctuation focuses on the use of variation of types of sentence, clarity, purpose and effect, and on grammatical accuracy and punctuation.

Text structure and organisation focuses on organising and presenting whole texts effectively, sequencing and structuring information, ideas and events, constructing paragraphs and using cohesion within and between paragraphs.

Composition and effect focuses on imaginative, interesting and thoughtful writing; writing a text which is suitable for its purpose and for the reader; and organising and presenting a text effectively.

The **Shorter Task** is assessed for **Sentence structure, punctuation and text organisation** (up to 4 marks) and **Composition and effect** (up to 8 marks). (Total 12 marks.)

Handwriting is assessed within the Longer Task (up to 3 marks).

Spelling is assessed in a separate test (20 marks).

The mark schemes each year are specific to the tests; new level thresholds are set for each year's tests to ensure that standards are maintained each year.

The conversion charts to National Curriculum levels provided on page 53 of this book should be regarded as a rough guide only.

Writing Test

Your child should first have read the passages in the Reading Tests.

Allow **45 minutes** for the **fiction** writing task and **20 minutes** for the **non-fiction** writing task.

An indication of National Curriculum levels is given on page 53.

FICTION (Longer Task): Introduce the planning sheet and read the starting point aloud. Discuss the headings on the sheet. Emphasise the importance of:

- writing a whole story and not just part of it;
- planning the story;
- thinking of a good opening to make the reader want to read on;
- keeping the reader interested;
- introducing the setting, the main character and the plot early in the story;
- helping the reader to get to know the characters;
- thinking of a good ending, rather than stopping abruptly.

NON-FICTION (Shorter Task): Discuss the points on the planning sheet. Emphasise the importance of:

- thinking up a good introduction to make the reader want to read on;
- keeping the reader interested;
- making the text easy for the reader to follow;
- thinking of a good ending so that the information does not just 'tail off'.

For both tasks, point out that grammar, spelling and punctuation are important.

If your child finishes before the allotted time is up, encourage him or her to read through what he or she has written to look for anything which can be improved and to check grammar, spelling and punctuation.

Fiction Writing Test
Planning Sheet

Making sense of Christmas

Read the extract from *Her Benny* and the poem 'They're Fetching in Ivy and Holly'. Write a story from the point of view of a visitor from another planet who has observed people celebrating Christmas and is trying to make sense of what he or she observes.

You have 45 minutes. Spend about 10 to 15 minutes of this time planning what you will write. Use the planning guidelines below.

Title

Setting
Where does the story take place?

When does it take place?

Characters
Name them and make notes about their personal qualities and characteristics.

Who is the main character or the narrator?

Who are the other characters?

Opening
Think of an opening which sets the scene and interests the reader.

Middle
Plan this section in paragraphs: what is each paragraph about?

Ending
How does the story end?

Have you forgotten anything?

Non-Fiction Writing Test
Planning Sheet

Christmas celebrations in the United Kingdom

Write a report for a website about the ways in which people in the United Kingdom celebrate Christmas.

You have 20 minutes. Spend about 5 to 10 minutes planning what you will write. Use the planning guidelines below.

On a flow-chart like this write everything you know about the ways in which people celebrate Christmas in the United Kingdom. Use arrows to begin to organise the pieces of information. This will help you to think of suitable sub-headings.

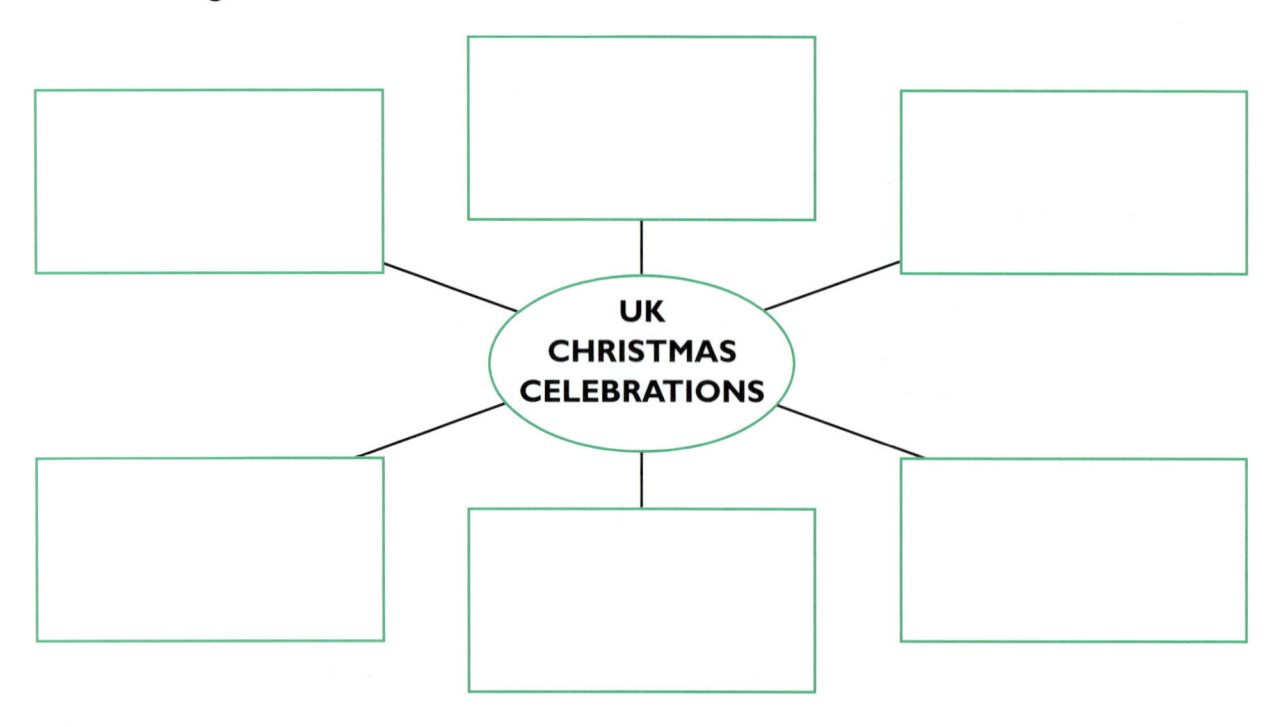

UK CHRISTMAS CELEBRATIONS

Decide in which person you should write ('we…' or 'they…'), how formal or informal your writing should be, and whether it should be mainly active or passive ('we do this' or 'this is done').

Make notes of useful words or phrases.

Make notes of useful connective words.

Plan the contents of each paragraph.

Think of a suitable introduction and conclusion.

Spelling Test
Instructions

Spelling

The Spelling Test contains words which are generally known at the end of Key Stage 2; they include many of the spelling strategies, conventions and rules suggested for Year 6 in the National Literacy Strategy *Framework for Teaching*.

> **This test is a short passage with words missed out.**
>
> **You read aloud from page 53 (the answers) – copy the text for ease of use.**
>
> **Your child should write on page 48.**
>
> **Allow 10 minutes for the Spelling Test.**
>
> **At the end of the test, give a mark for each correct word and enter it in the space provided.**
>
> **National Curriculum levels are given on page 53.**

1 Ask your child to listen to you reading the complete text.

2 Ask the child to look at his or her copy of the text. Point out that some of the words have been left out.

3 Tell your child that you are going to read the text again and that he or she should write in the missing words as you read. The missing words are in bold type on your copy of the text (page 53).

4 Read the text aloud again, pausing after each word in bold type, to give your child time to write it on the test copy. You can repeat each of the bold words up to three times, if necessary.

Spelling Test

Where did Christmas cards _____ ?

This _____ way of _____ seasonal _____ began in the nineteenth _____.

An artist named W C T Dodgson is _____ to have made and sent the first Christmas card, in 1844. It led to the _____ of the first _____ Christmas card by Sir Henry Cole and J C Horsley in 1846. The card showed members of a _____ enjoying a glass of wine (a wassail cup): this was _____ by the Temperance Society, which was doing a great deal of work in cities like Manchester, Leeds and London to _____ people not to drink _____. By the 1870s, _____ cards were _____. They included _____ Christmas _____, symbols such as holly, _____, mistletoe, _____ and _____, as well as the Nativity: the stable, angels and _____.

TOTAL 20

Answers
Reading Test

Question number	Answer	Mark
INFORMATION: CHRISTMAS CELEBRATIONS		
1	Mexico, Sweden, Nicaragua and Jamaica.	2 (1 mark if two or three are named)
2	The processions in Nicaragua and Mexico. In Nicaragua, people sing hymns to the Virgin Mary. In Mexico, the processions enact Mary and Joseph's search for somewhere to stay.	2 2
3	Sweden.	1
4	The Yule log and St Lucia's Day in Sweden and the *Jolasveinar* in Iceland.	3
5	Gnomes or elves bring gifts *or* they end on 6 January.	1
6	They made Christmas products for other countries.	1
7	Iceland and Japan. In Iceland, the elves leave presents only for children who have been good; if they have been naughty the elves leave a potato or some other reminder to behave themselves. In Japan, Santa watches what they are doing all through the year.	1 2
8	Nicaragua.	1
9	Yule festivals are about light and warmth. Saint Lucia was a Christian martyr who had a wreath of candles to light her way along dark passages.	3 marks for a complete answer. 1 mark if light is mentioned.
10	In Iceland, the *Jolasveinar* leave on 6 January, and in Sweden the Yule log is burned until 6 January.	2
FICTION: HER BENNY		
1	There was too much choice.	1
2	The person they lived with.	1
3	The food.	1
4	They didn't know who Christ was.	1
5	She didn't know how or where to begin telling them the story of Christ.	1
6	I expect.	1
7	No. They cannot read *or* they have never heard the story of the Nativity.	1 1
8	By golly! By jabbers! Golly! I's sold!	1 mark for each. Maximum 3.
9	He is stressing that *he* knows how Betty can read the story from the page *or* It is the same as saying 'I'll eat my hat …'	1
10	Is I?, I thinks, folks is, Wur it, you was, I's got it, it's the specks that does it, I's sold!, this are. Gooses. You was. Ain't you never heerd?	2 marks for four. 1 mark for one to three. 1 1 1
11	I specks (I expect), specks (glasses/spectacles), dunna (do not/don't), 'polish off' (eat), 'ee (you), ain't (are not/have not), dunno (don't know), nowt (nothing)	2 marks for four, 1 mark for one to three.
12	Busy and full of Christmas foods. 'Crowds of people' and lists of the things the children see, with words which give the impression of large amounts, like thousands, heaps, tons and loads.	1 1
13	Stalls of sweetmeats, tons of toffee, bent upon buying.	2 marks for all three. 1 mark for one or two.
14	Benny was impressed by the way Betty could read a story from the marks on the pages, but Nelly was fascinated by the story itself.	2
15	He does not use normal spelling, but spells the words in the way in which people said them: ud 'ave (would have), o' (of), dunna (don't), dunno (don't know), an' (and), yer (you), wur (were), heerd (heard), nuthin (nothing), mebbe (maybe), bizness (business).	1 1 mark for four examples.
16	He is a Christian. He calls the story of Christ 'the wonderful story'. The story suggests that the children ought to know about it.	1 2 marks for both observations; 1 mark for one of them.
POETRY: THEY'RE FETCHING IN IVY AND HOLLY		
1	It mentions: holly and ivy; people pinning up lanterns and streamers; mistletoe; a tree covered with glass candles and with a fairy on top; cards; carol singers; children posting letters up the chimney to Santa Claus.	1 mark each. Maximum 3.
2	Yes. It can't think of the reason. It asks someone to tell it.	1 2
3	That children posted letters up the chimney.	1
4	I simply can't think of a reason … I do wish I knew what it's for, I couldn't believe my own eyes … Won't somebody come and tell me?	1 mark for each. Maximum 3.
5	Nothing. There is no mention of the Nativity or Christ.	2
6	Their actions have nothing to do with Christmas *or* At Christmas people go mad/ lose their senses/ do silly things. *or* Christmas has no real meaning for some people.	3

49

Answers
Writing Test

The **Longer Task** is assessed for the following:

Sentence structure and punctuation (up to 8 marks) – focuses on the use of variation of types of sentence, clarity, purpose and effect, and on grammatical accuracy and punctuation.

Text structure and organisation (up to 8 marks) – focuses on organising and presenting whole texts effectively, sequencing and structuring information, ideas and events, constructing paragraphs and using cohesion within and between paragraphs.

Composition and effect (up to 12 marks) – focuses on imaginative, interesting and thoughtful writing; writing a text which is suitable for its purpose and for the reader; and organising and presenting (including handwriting) a text effectively. (Total 28 marks.)

The **Shorter Task** is assessed for **Sentence structure, punctuation and text organisation** (up to 4 marks) and **Composition and effect** (up to 8 marks). (Total 12 marks.)

Longer Task (Fiction)

Sentence structure and punctuation	Marks
Joins parts of sentences mostly with *and* and *but*. Uses some simple sentences, mainly simple grammatically accurate statements in the past tense. Sometimes demarcates sentences with capital letters and full stops.	1
Uses a limited range of time connectives: *and* and *then* to link clauses. Subjects and verbs are frequently repeated; use of modal verbs: for example, *should, would*. Noun phrases mostly simple (for example, *a number, the Christmas tree*) with occasional expansion (for example, *stocking masks*). Sometimes includes generalising words: for example, *every, only*. Uses full stops, capital letters, exclamation marks and question marks to demarcate sentences, mostly accurately; uses commas in lists.	2–3
Develops explanation within sentences through using subordinating connectives (*if, because*). Varies the construction of sentences using adverbials (for example, *at the end of the day*) and expanded noun phrases (for example, *the bright, shining star*). Uses verb tenses consistently in most cases. There is some correct use of commas within sentences to mark phrases or clauses.	4–5
Uses simple and complex sentences, with some variety of connectives: for example, the subordinating conjunctions *which* and *who*. Uses expanded phrases and clauses to express ideas economically (*presents wrapped in shining paper*). Uses the appropriate tenses of verbs: present, past, future and, where necessary, conditionals. Qualifying words and phrases (*a little better, too much, amazingly bright*) contribute to precision. Almost all sentences are correctly demarcated with a range of punctuation: for example, brackets, dashes and colons.	6–7
Varies the lengths and focuses of sentences to express shades of meaning: for example, might use passives (*socks and pillowcases were hung up*). Word order may be manipulated for emphasis: for example, *lastly, and most importantly*. Sentences may include embedded subordinate clauses for economy of expression: for example, *We were amazed, watching their feast, when the pudding was set on fire*. Uses a range of punctuation correctly (full stops, commas, colons, semi-colons, question marks, exclamation marks and dashes), with little omission, to mark the structure of sentences and texts and to give clarity.	8

Writing Test Answers

Text structure and organisation	Marks
Groups ideas into sequences of sentences, with some division possibly indicated by layout: for example, line breaks or boxes might be used. The organisation of the argument might be chronological rather than logical. Uses simple connectives (*and, but*). There is some connection between sentences: for example, through the use of pronouns referring to the same thing (*he/she/it, they, that boy, those houses*).	1
Simple overall text structure includes brief introduction or concluding statement (for example, *That is how we came to have fir trees on our planet*). Indicates some divisions between sections of the content: sub-headings, use of *also* for additional information (*there are also*) and paragraphs. Relationships between ideas in the argument are usually non-chronological, similar ideas usually being grouped together. Uses pronouns to make connections between sentences, by referring to people or things in the previous sentence: for example, *he, she, it, they, their*.	2–3
The structure of the text includes an introduction, chronologically ordered points (or using 'flashback' to break from the chronology) and a conclusion. Consistently indicates new sections by new paragraphs; uses introductory phrases. If used, conventional phrases are integrated into the text (*after some time, the next day, the last night*).	4–5
Relationships between paragraphs give a structure to the whole text: for example, connections make the structure clear to the reader by referring forwards and backwards (for example, *After doing this/What it symbolised was*). Develops paragraphs: creates a convincing recount through the use of details.	6–7
Sequencing of sections contributes to overall effectiveness of text: for example, by placing the most interesting or appealing idea to give maximum impact. The story might begin with a sentence, or even a paragraph, which attracts attention before going on to recount the story. Varies the length and structure of paragraphs, giving each paragraph a clear focus, and organising the content by reference within and between paragraphs.	8
Composition and effect	
Writes a short series of sentences recounting events. There is some attempt to interest the reader: for example, by using dialogue.	1–2
Indicates shifts of time through the use of time connectives such as *afterwards, the next morning*. The writing shows evidence of an attempt to create an atmosphere or mood. There is evidence that the writer has tried to write in a specific style: formal or informal, as appropriate to the reader and context.	3–5
Adapts the narrative form in the past tense to the situation: for example, the content is informative; the details are well placed to present a clear recount. The writer's viewpoint is established and maintained: for example, the writing suggests the writer's concern or amusement, as appropriate.	6–8
Adapts ideas to suit the intended readers. Establishes and controls a clear and consistent style. Maintains the reader's interest through the use of stylistic devices such as synonyms to avoid repetition (*soon/before long, huge/massive/vast, hardly anyone/scarcely anyone/few people*). Interesting or exciting vocabulary keeps the reader's attention.	9–11
The writer's choice of content and the way in which it is arranged are suited to the intended readers: for example, through the use of appropriate vocabulary and language level. The writer's viewpoint is well controlled and convincing.	12

Writing Test Answers

Shorter Task (Non-Fiction)

Sentence structure, punctuation and text organisation	Marks
Uses some simple sentences, mainly simple grammatically accurate statements in the present tense. Usually starts with the third person: for example, *They bring a small tree into the house.* Uses capital letters to begin most sentences and full stops to end them. Clauses are usually grammatically accurate, mostly joined with *and*, *but* and *then*. May use simple repetition for emphasis (for example, *a long, long way*; *very, very big*). Makes some connections between sentences: for example, through the use of pronouns referring back to people or things (*it/they*).	1
Uses the first or third person and the present tense consistently. Writes mostly compound sentences, with clauses linked by connectives such as *and*, *but* and *so*. Uses simple adjectives such as *big, good, small*. Uses full stops and capital letters accurately. Might use commas in lists. Uses apostrophes accurately. Uses simple adjectives, such as *good, long, wide, old*. Often repeats subjects and verbs (*it had, it was*). Clauses are mostly joined with *and*, *but* and *or*, with some use of *if*. Expands some sentences with simple adverbials, such as *slowly, upwards*. Sometimes makes explicit the relationships between sentences or clauses, for example through giving additional information.	2
Uses grammatically accurate clauses. Uses some imaginative adjectives, such as *enormous, glittering*. Might use comparative or superlative adjectives such as *better, best, neater, neatest*. Varies the sentence construction: adverbials (*down the chimney, on top of the tree*) and expanded noun phrases (*strings of sparkling tinsel, a sweet-smelling fir tree*) to add detail. Uses some subordinating connectives, such as *if* and *when*. Some commas mark phrases or clauses.	3
Varies the sentence lengths. Qualifies adjectives with adverbs such as *fairly, quite, very*. Uses some of the more sophisticated punctuation marks where appropriate: semi-colons, colons, dashes, ellipses. Uses compound and complex sentences with varied connectives, for example, *which* and *although*, and varied sentence constructions for effect: for example, using passives to alter the focus of attention and short sentences for emphasis.	4
Composition and effect	
Groups some of the ideas into sets of sentences. Sometimes the layout helps to split ideas into groups (for example, starting on a new line, writing in a box, using a sub-heading).	1
Includes a range of relevant details, in which some parts are grouped by topic, but this grouping might not be consistent. Indicates some divisions between sections of the content: for example, by using headings, line breaks or paragraphing.	2–3
Introduces an opinion or point of view (but might not maintain it): for example, description in the first or third person.	4–5
Maintains a point of view (for example, description in the first or third person) for most of the writing.	6–7
Maintains a point of view (for example, description in the first or third person) throughout the text. Tailors the text to the reader (for example, through the use of appropriate vocabulary). The voice of the writer is well controlled and convincing: for example, the writer adopts a persona whose character becomes apparent as the account of the experience unfolds. Manipulates stylistic devices to support the purpose fully and to entertain the audience: for example, figurative language, such as comparisons, similes and metaphors.	8

Answers
Spelling Test

Where did Christmas cards **originate**? This **popular** way of **exchanging** seasonal **greetings** began in the nineteenth **century**. An artist named W C T Dodgson is **thought** to have made and sent the first Christmas card, in 1844. It led to the **production** of the first **commercial** Christmas card by Sir Henry Cole and J C Horsley in 1846. The card showed members of a **family** enjoying a glass of wine (a wassail cup): this was **condemned** by the Temperance Society, which was doing a great deal of work in cities like Manchester, Leeds and London to **persuade** people not to drink **alcohol**. By the 1870s, **manufactured** cards were **commonplace**. They included **traditional** Christmas **scenes**, symbols such as holly, **ivy**, mistletoe, **lanterns** and **candles**, as well as the Nativity: the stable, angels and **shepherds**.

National Curriculum Levels
English

Use the conversion tables below to gain an idea of your child's National Curriculum level.

Information Reading	
Mark	Level
0–3	Below Level 2
4–7	Level 2
8–12	Level 3
13–18	Level 4
19–21	Level 5

Fiction Reading	
Mark	Level
0–5	Below Level 2
6–12	Level 2
13–21	Level 3
22–26	Level 4
27–30	Level 5

Poetry Reading	
0–2	Below Level 2
3–6	Level 2
7–10	Level 3
11–13	Level 4
14–15	Level 5

Spelling	
0–3	Below Level 3
4–6	Level 3
7–14	Level 4
15–20	Level 5

Writing
Write your child's marks here:

Spelling	
Writing Longer Task	
Writing Shorter Task	
Total	

Approximate National Curriculum Levels

Marks	0–9	10–29	30–47	48–60
Level	Below Level 3	3	4	5

If your child needs more practice in any English topics, use the WHSmith Key Stage 2 English Revision Guide.

Science

Science at Key Stage 2

Most children at Key Stage 2 attain Levels 3 to 4 in Science, but some may attain Level 5.

This performance at the different levels is summarised below.

Level 3	Level 4	Level 5
Children can describe differences and provide simple explanations. They can sort materials and living things and offer ideas about why materials are suitable for their purpose. When explaining how things work they link cause and effect, such as suggesting that the lack of light causes plants to become yellow. They also make generalisations about things they see, such as suggesting that it is difficult to see dim lights if they are near very bright lights.	Children can use more scientific terms such as the names of the organs of the body and those of flowering plants. They can use technical terms to describe processes such as evaporation and condensation. They can explain how differences are used to classify materials and living things systematically. They use their ideas about the way the physical world works when explaining how shadows are formed or the way that sound is heard through different materials.	Children can explain the factors behind why different organisms are found in different environments. They can describe the properties of metals and how they are distinct from other materials. They can identify why changes occur in materials and can suggest ways in which specific mixtures can be separated. They can use abstract ideas and models to explain physical phenomena such as the orbiting model of the earth to explain day and year length.

Setting the test

Give your child plenty of time to do the test – 45 minutes should be about right.

The test can be a chance to confirm how well your child has done and how much he or she has learnt. Don't focus exclusively on what the child does not know.

Enter the mark in the circle next to each question. Add the marks together at the end of the test. Look at page 64 for an indication of the level at which your child is working.

Science Test

Shadows

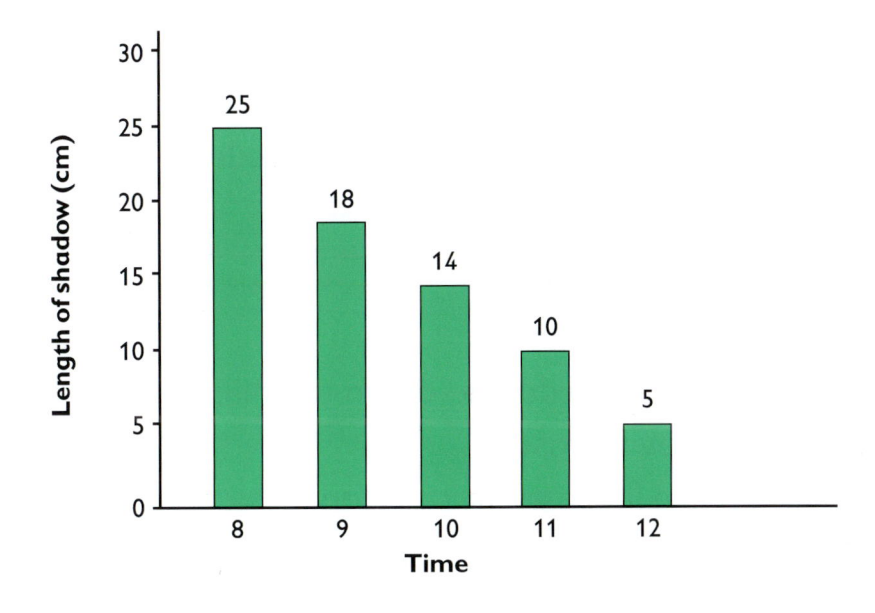

1 Some children put a stick in the ground.
They record its length at different times of the day.
They put their results on a graph.

[Bar graph: Length of shadow (cm) vs Time — 8: 25, 9: 18, 10: 14, 11: 10, 12: 5]

a What makes the length of the shadow alter during the day?

_____

_____

b How else does the shadow change?

Tick one answer.

It gets thicker. ☐

It moves round the stick. ☐

It gets darker. ☐

TOTAL 2

55

Science Test

Forces

2 Kerrie is checking her bike.
She checks to make sure that the brakes are rubbing on the wheels to make them stop quickly.

    a What is the force which slows the bike down?
    _____

1

    b One wheel is stiff so she oils the axle.
    How does this help?
    _____

1

    c Kerrie is not pedalling down the hill.
    She is moving fast.
    Draw the force of air resistance acting on this bike.

1

The water cycle

3 Add the correct word to each sentence to explain the water cycle.

    evaporates   vapour   rain   condenses   flow

4

Water falls as _____ and runs into rivers.

Rivers _____ to the sea.

Water _____ into the air.

Water _____ is an invisible gas in the air.

Vapour _____ to form a cloud.

TOTAL

7

Science Test

Mixtures

4 Some cereals are mixtures of bran, oats and dried fruit. Bill and Ben separated two such cereal mixtures.

a Circle **two** things they could use for this.

They put the bran, the oats and the dried fruit from each cereal in different piles and weighed them.
They recorded their results on pie charts:

Cereal A: 100 g   Cereal B: 100 g

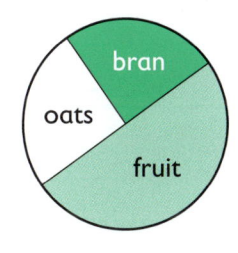

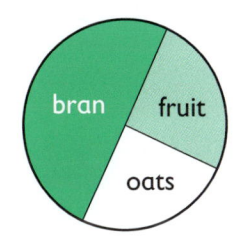

b

	Cereal A	Cereal B
What fraction of the cereal was bran?		
What weight of the cereal was bran?		

c Fruit tastes sweet.

Which cereal would taste sweeter?

_____

d They mixed milk with each cereal. After an hour the milk had disappeared and the cereal had expanded.

What had happened?

_____

1

2

1

1

TOTAL

5

57

Science Test

Materials

5 a Sunil is making toffee. He has a wooden spoon or a metal spoon to stir the hot mixture. Which one should he use?

_____

b Explain your answer.

_____

_____

c Masie needs to take some cakes out of the oven. She has rubber gloves or fabric gloves to wear.

Which should she use?

_____

d Explain your answer.

_____

_____

6 Hamish and Lara are making sandcastles. Hamish has a full bucket of wet sand. Lara has a full bucket of dry sand. Both buckets are the same size.
Explain why Hamish's bucket feels heavier than Lara's.

_____

_____

Food chains

7 Link the correct boxed label to each part of food chain below. Use each word only once.

| prey | producer | predator | consumer |

lettuce → snail → thrush → cat

TOTAL: 9

Science Test

Fish tank

8 Tim measured the temperature of the water in his fish tank. He used a sensor attached to a computer to record the changes.

This is Tim's temperature chart.

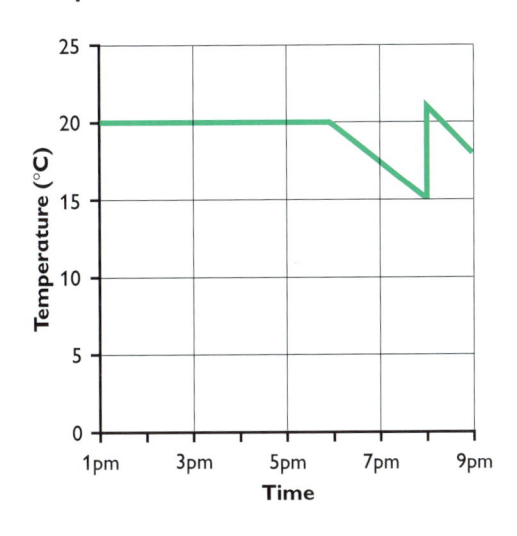

a How long was the sensor in the tank?

_____

b What was the temperature of the water in the tank at first?

_____

c What was the temperature of the water at 9 pm?

_____

d Tim added some warm water to the tank. At what time did he do this?

_____

e Fish tanks are made from glass or plastic. Give **two** reasons why these materials are used.

_____

_____

Science Test

Plants

9 a Write a question which will help Sam to put these leaves into two different groups.

_____

_____

b John has listed the stages in the life cycle of a plant. They are in the wrong order.

Number the sentences to show which order they should be in.
(The first has been done for you.)

The flowers are pollinated. ☐

The seeds are dispersed. [1]

A root grows down. ☐

The plant grows and produces flowers. ☐

New seeds develop. ☐

Science Test

Temperature

10 a Amy and Dan are looking at the way in which ice cubes melt.

Amy thinks that the amount of light falling on the cubes is important. Dan thinks the temperature of the air around the cubes is important.

Write how you could test Amy's idea.

_____

_____

_____

2

Write how you could test Dan's idea.

_____

_____

_____

2

b Which things would you keep the same in the tests for Amy's idea?

_____

_____

2

Which things would you keep the same in the tests for Dan's idea?

_____

_____

2

TOTAL

8

Science Test

Temperature

c Amy and Dan also test how quickly one ice cube melts in water at different temperatures.

Here is the graph they made.

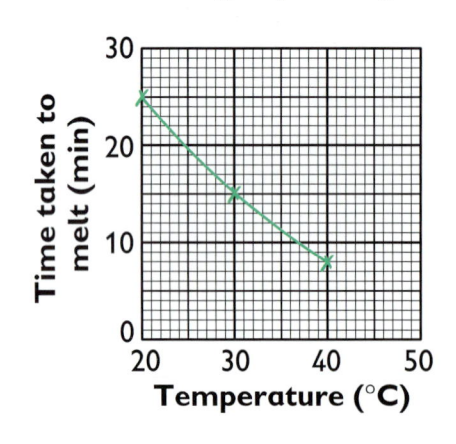

Use the graph to help.

How long did it take for the ice cube to melt in water at 30 °C?

_____

How long did it take for the ice cube to melt in water at 40 °C?

_____

d Amy and Dan want to time how long they can keep an ice pop frozen. They are going to try different places.

Put these places in order to show which you think will keep the ice pop frozen for longest.

Number the places. **1** is the place where it will stay frozen for longest. It has been done for you.

putting one on a sunny windowsill	
putting one in the freezer	1
putting one in a fridge	
putting one in a cool cupboard	
putting one in hot water	

TOTAL

Answers
Science Test

Question number	Answer	Mark
1a	The earth spinning on its axis makes the length of the shadow alter. *or* The movement of the sun across the sky makes the shadow alter.	1
1b	It moves round the stick.	1
2a	Friction	1
2b	It reduces friction. *or* It lubricates the axle.	1
2c	The arrow can be at any height above the ground, but must be in the opposite direction to the movement of the bike.	1
3	Water falls as rain and runs into rivers. Rivers flow to the sea. Water evaporates into the air. Water vapour is an invisible gas in the air. Vapour condenses to form a cloud.	4
4a	The sieve and the colander could be circled.	1
4b	Cereal A: The fraction of bran was one-quarter (1/4). The weight of bran was 25 g. Cereal B: The fraction of bran was one-half (1/2). The weight of bran was 50 g.	2 ($\frac{1}{2}$ mark for each answer)
4c	Cereal A would taste sweeter.	1
4d	The milk had been absorbed by the cereal.	1
5a	wooden	1
5b	The metal spoon would get too hot (because it is a good conductor of heat). *or* The wooden spoon would stay cool because it is a poor conductor of heat.	1
5c	fabric	1
5d	The rubber ones might melt. *or* The fabric ones will not conduct heat so well. *or* The fabric gloves will insulate better.	1
6	There is water in with the sand.	1
7	lettuce – producer snail – consumer thrush – prey cat – predator	4
8a	8 hours	1
8b	20 °C	1
8c	Approx 18 °C	1
8d	8 pm	1
8e	Plastic and glass are transparent *or* see-through and strong *or* do not conduct heat.	2
9a	Is the leaf in one piece? *or* Is the leaf made up from small parts? Accept other suitable questions.	1
9b	The flowers are pollinated – 4 The seeds are dispersed – 1 A root grows down – 2 The plant grows and produces flowers – 3 New seeds develop – 5	4

63

Science Test Answers

Question number	Answer	Mark

10a	**You might test Amy's idea by:**
	Where possible keeping the two cubes at the same temperature:
	    put one ice cube in a dark place and the other in a light place
	    or
	    put them both in the same light place and cover one with a box.
	You might test Dan's idea by:
	    Put one cube in a dark warm place and the other cube in a dark cool place
	    or
	    Put one cube in a light warm place and the other cube in a light cool place.
		2
		
		2

10b	**You would keep these things the same for Amy's idea:**
	Two of:
	    keep both cubes in places which were the same temperature;
	    have the cubes start as the same size;
	    keep them in similar containers.
	
	You would keep these things the same for Dan's idea:
	Two of:
	    keep both cubes in places which are lit the same;
	    have the cubes start as the same size;
	    keep them in similar containers.
		2 and 2

10c	30 °C took 15 mins 40 °C took 8 mins	1 1
10d	putting one on a sunny windowsill – 4 putting one in the freezer – 1 putting one in a fridge – 2 putting one in a cool cupboard – 3 putting one in hot water – 5	4

National Curriculum Levels

Science

Total marks 48

Mark	0–19	20–27	28–38	39–48
Level	Below Level 3	Level 3	Level 4	Level 5

If your child needs more practice in any Science topics, use the WHSmith Key Stage 2 Science Revision Guide.